A story to introduce 'Jupiter' by Holst

Editor: Robin Norman
Illustrations: Vanessa Lubach
Design and Layout: Glide Design
Cd recording issued under license from Sanctuary Records Group Ltd.

IMP
International
MUSIC
Publications

© International Music Publications Limited Griffin House 161 Hammersmith Road London W6 8BS England
Published 2004

BRING CLASSICAL MUSIC TO LIFE!
FOR HOME OR SCHOOL

"As the I.T. teacher in a primary school in New Zealand, I am constantly looking for material that will stimulate, interest and if I'm lucky, excite and inspire my students. I can honestly say that the six stories in this series have exceeded my expectations and I have found them to be one of the most valuable resources I have used to date.

The books have something to offer to children from years 1 to 8 (the full primary school age range here in New Zealand) and it never ceases to amaze me how much they inspire the children. The combination of story with illustration and music is a great I.T. resource and the children create descriptive text, as well as art work, within the computer art programs available, and slide shows ranging from simple to complex.

The wonderfully inventive language they use to describe their work is reflective of what they are seeing and hearing within the stories and now the children are requesting other classical music pieces for their own original creations. Fantastic!"

Sharon Gardner, I.T. Teacher
Koputaroa School, Levin, New Zealand

"Story time is always special, but what a wonderful experience this was! Our two young sons, aged 5 and 3, were completely captivated by this series. They were wide-eyed with delight as they were able to hear in the music what was happening in the stories.

After a number of listenings, they were able to hear the music telling the story and painting pictures in their heads. Afterwards, I was plagued with requests for more!

I hope that the series continues to expand as this is something I'm sure we can use again and again to build on the children's understanding and love of music."

Penny Hill, Parent
Bury St. Edmunds, Suffolk

ABOUT THE BOOK

These books are designed to be used as part of your scheme of work for music, literacy and art and will particularly help generalists, as they are straight forward, interesting and fun to use. At home they become a fantastic alternative to traditional storytime.

If you ask children what they think of classical music they often say "It's boring." That's an understandable reaction. Classical music doesn't have the 'immediacy' of pop, rock, rap etc. It lacks a constant, even beat, often lacks lyrics and is usually longer than the average pop song.

However pieces such as The Sorcerer's Apprentice usually prove very popular with young children. Why? Because they have strong contrasting dynamics, are very descriptive, and best of all, they have a story. It is the

story, particularly when combined with illustrations, that is the instant attraction.

Many pieces of classical music either do not have a story at all, or have an inappropriate one – too old, too complicated, too scary or simply too uninteresting. This series uses original stories written specifically for young children and inspired by short interesting pieces of music from a variety of different cultures. Although the stories are original, they bear some association with the title and flavour of the music.

HOW TO USE THIS BOOK AND CD

- Play the CD straight through and read the story at the same time

- In the book you will see a number of CD counter indications. This tells you when to proceed to the next part of the story

- Alternatively read the story through first then play the CD and this time just look at the pictures so you feel suspended by the music in the story

- Enjoy!

About 'Jupiter' from 'The Planets Suite'

Holst was an English composer. He lived from 1874 – 1934. He was descended from a family of mixed Scandinavian, German and Russian origin. The Planets is an orchestral suite which was completed in 1916, but it was not until 1920 that the first public performance took place and proved a wonderful triumph. It is one of the loudest pieces of music ever written, and in parts one of the quietest. It is also one of the most popular choices for concert-goers.

There are seven movements with astrological titles, loosely based on the characters and moods of the Roman Gods after which the planets were named – Mars, the Bringer of War; Venus, the Bringer of Peace; Mercury, the Winged Messenger; Jupiter, the Bringer of Jollity; Saturn, the Bringer of Old Age; Uranus, the Magician; and Neptune, the Mystic. Pluto was not a known planet at the time that Holst wrote his composition, and he chose to leave out the planet Earth.

Jupiter is the ruler of the Gods. In this section you will hear a wild dance in three time and also the solemn tune which was subsequently used for the hymn *I Vow to Thee My Country*. Holst might have thought of The Planets as a progression of life with Jupiter representing the prime of life.

Now enjoy the story!

Ollie and his friends spent all their time playing on the beach amongst the rocks. Every day they went a little further and a little further, discovering more and more interesting places to explore...

CD ON

...until one day Ollie found himself on the edge of
Jupiter Cove. He stood on the highest rock of all. It
was completely flat, and gleamed pale gold as though
the sun had polished its smooth vast surface.

"Look!" he called. "Over here! It's brilliant!"

The others clambered and scrambled over
the massive boulders to join Ollie.

00.40

"Wow!" breathed Ella. "You can see for miles."

00.50

Then a wave slapped against a rock below, sending
an arc of salty water spraying over them.

01.07

The children laughed and lay on their stomachs,
peering over the edge of the rock. Waves were
plipping and sploshing a long way below,
and the sea spray fizzed everywhere.

01.24

"Ssh!" said Danny. "I can hear something...   It's coming from under the water."

Ella's eyes widened. "Perhaps it's a submarine."

01.42

"What's that?" said Ollie, pointing with a trembling finger.

In the distance the sea was changing colour. The children gasped and their eyes grew big, as a patch of grey seeped into the blue.

Then another.

And another.

The shapes seemed to be drawing nearer and nearer, faster and faster.

"Quick!" said Ollie.

And there was a rush to clamber down
to the rocks below, where there were
hiding places and peep holes.

02.39

It was hard not to gasp as strange dark creatures rose up out of the sea. Up and up and up.

"Giant sea horses!" breathed Danny.

The others could only stare.

03.10

Slowly and grandly, like massive patrolling guards, the creatures began to move around the rocks of Jupiter Cove. And as they moved, the sea rose and fell, swaying and lilting in time with them.

03.35

The children watched from below in wide eyed silence. From the throats of the creatures came a low singing noise, as they took turns to lay great strands of slime-oozing seaweed on to the smooth surface of the high rock.

04.13

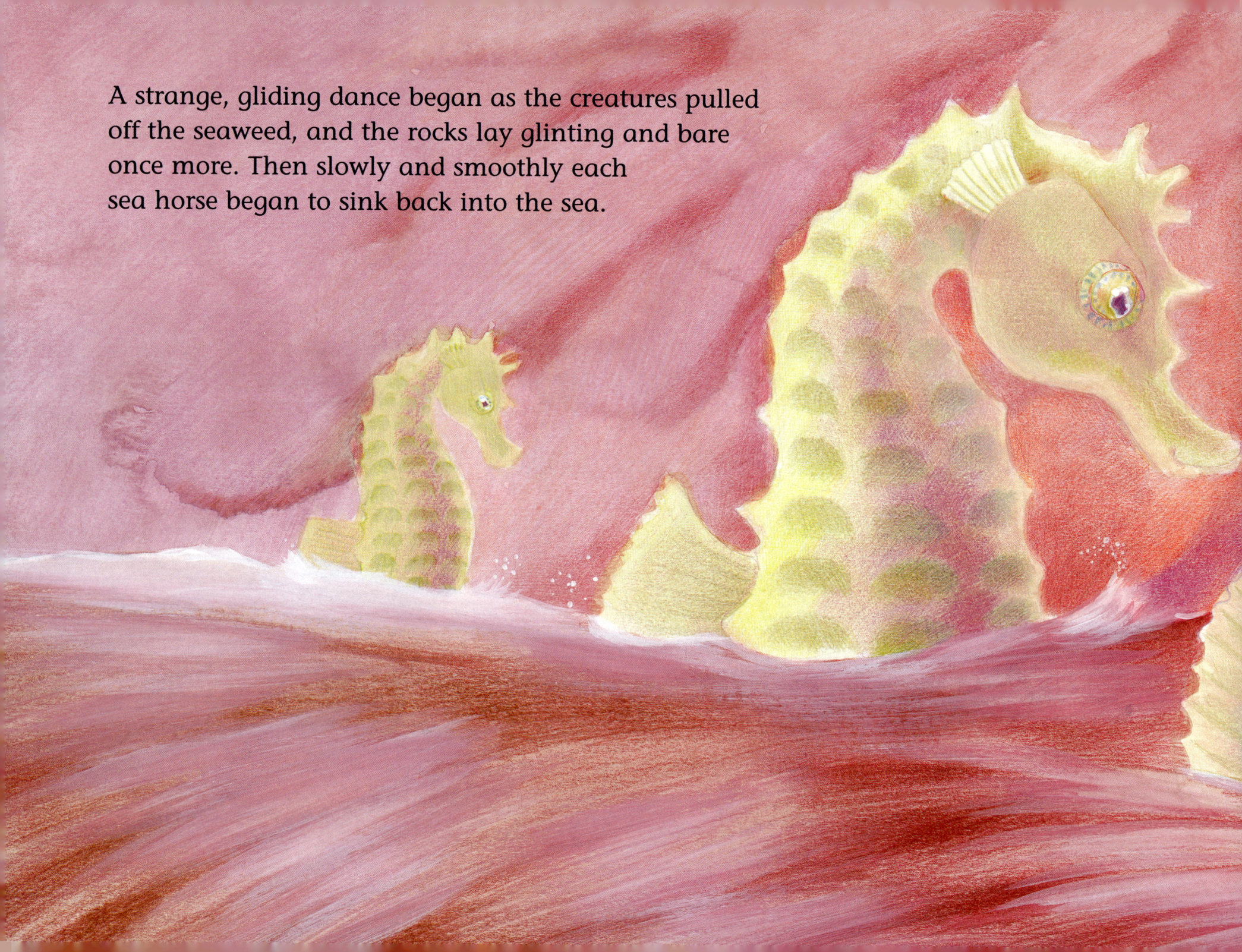

A strange, gliding dance began as the creatures pulled off the seaweed, and the rocks lay glinting and bare once more. Then slowly and smoothly each sea horse began to sink back into the sea.

Gradually the water folded over the heads of the sea horses, leaving only the smudgy grey patches. And eventually even they dissolved back into blue.

04.57

The children shivered.

"Did that really happen?" Ella asked in a frightened whisper.

Neither Danny nor Ollie had an answer. They were too wrapped up in their thoughts.

05.17

"Look!" said Danny. "The sea! It's rising! We've got to get away!"

"Right now!" Ella added. "It's happening so fast!"

05.40

Danny started to inch backwards, keeping his eyes on the surging sea. "The whole cove will be covered soon."

06.01

The three children stood on the beach and looked towards the place where they had been standing only moments before.

"We were so lucky," breathed Ella.

"And what became of the sea horses?" asked Danny. "*Or did* we imagine them?"

"Oh they were there, all right," said Ollie. "Don't you get it? They were warning us of the danger, making the rock slippery with seaweed so we wouldn't be able to go back up there."

Ella spoke slowly as she scanned the sea. "They saved our lives, didn't they. And now they've gone, we can't even thank them."

"Yes we can," said Ollie. And he cupped his hands round his mouth and yelled out, "Thanks for the warning!"

The others joined in, jumping up and down, waving their arms and shouting out to sea at the tops of their voices, "Thanks for the warning! Thanks for the warning!"

07.21

And from somewhere in the depths of the ocean came a familiar noise. A deep throaty song. The children couldn't believe their ears.

07.40

Ollie broke into a smile.
"Yesss!" he cried triumphantly.
"They heard us!"

END